BOSS MOVES:

WHAT THEY DIDN'T TEACH YOU IN BEAUTY SCHOOL

By Amber Hopson

Table Of Contents

CUSTOMER SERVICE

RESPECT TIME AND IT WILL RESPECT
YOU

ANSWER YO DAMN PHONE

BAD ASSOCIATIONS SPOIL USEFUL
HABITS

DEDICATION

I would like to dedicate this book to my son, Solomon. He will always be my motivation to be the very best in everything I do.

INTRODUCTION

The sole purpose of cosmetology school is to prepare you for the State Board Cosmetology Test. Once you pass the State Board, what's next? Some go off to be assistants in a hair salon to build their skills and to learn the business. Others may work at a salon on a junior level and do commission. You also have stylists like myself who already have salon experience and just need their license to be legit. Whatever the case may be, a successful stylist needs to not only be skilled at their craft, but needs to know the nature of the business.

After beauty school, you're thrown to the wolves without a survival kit. In this book, we will explore several strategies to assist you in your journey:

- How to build your brand

- Tips on how to gain clients

- How to keep clients

- Financial literacy: How to save money

- Finally, but most importantly, how to maintain your business and become a successful business owner.

Through experience, trial and error; I learned about the beauty business. Also, I've gained insight by observing how other stylists and salon owners, whether successful or ineffective, conducted business. I observed more ways on how to ruin a salon business than how to keep one alive. Case in point, all eight salons that I had the opportunity to work at are all out of business except for one. That one exception downgraded from a store front salon to a suite. This isn't to put anyone down, but I brought this up to say that it is very difficult to not only run a business but to stay in business; it is not for everybody.

<u>ABOUT ME</u>

On Saturdays, while my peers were eating cereal and watching their favorite cartoons, I was going door to door with my mother selling Jehovah's Witness material. My early grind was real…waking up most people out of their sleep. Can you imagine doors slammed in your face, getting cursed out, getting chased by dogs and you're only knee high? Well, that was my experience of rejection dating back to my early years. After a while, I built a callous on my feelings, not letting anyone or thing discourage me from making a sale.

I started to appreciate the hustle, since my mother would let me keep the money I made from the publications I sold. Not knowing then, I was being groomed for entrepreneurship. I can remember learning to bake sweet potato pies from one of the elderly ladies from our congregation. Once I mastered the recipe, off I went selling pies to neighbors and church goers for $12.

My great-great grandmother, Neneh, would play country and western music while she teaching me how to crochet. It was a great way for us to bond and learn a trade. Fast forward to when I was a starving student, attending El Camino college; living on my own. I took my crochet skills that Neneh taught me and sold crochet accessories like scarves and beanies to students on campus.

At an early age, I taught myself how to braid while playing with Barbie's. Even though I developed a knack for hair, it was not my passion. In fact, it was just something that came easy to me. Deriving from a musically inclined family, it was natural for me to pursue music. My mom would perform at weddings to make extra money on the side and of course, she dragged me with her. I watched her work a 9 to 5 and do side hustles such as, teach piano lessons, play her violin in orchestras, and she even did a mobile nail service.

A couple of years after high school, my rapping career took off, landing me a record deal with an all- girl rap group called "Da 5footaz". We were signed to Warren G's production company in the mid Nineties. I had the opportunity to tour across the Country; performing in front of thousands of people. We recorded and performed with dozens of famous artists, like Nate Dogg, the Dogg Pound, MC Lyte, The Outlaws, just to name a few. At 21, I bought my first car, a red BMW when I received my first royalty check from a song (The Heist) from the "Set It Off," movie soundtrack.

I was in love with music, but I hated the music business. I would have to write a separate book, just on the music industry to share all of those experiences. At 23, I delivered a son into this world, Solomon Maeshack. While being signed to a record company, I ended up applying for welfare to feed my son. I knew at that point in my life, that I had to change the game. Timing is everything!

I had no idea that being a hairstylist would ever be my future career. I enrolled in school in 2003, while my music career was on hiatus. Attending school full time, with no job, and raising a young son was very difficult for me. Thank God for section 8 and all of the other government assistance that I utilized.

During those trying times, I made a way out of no way. I invested in a salon chair and started doing hair out of my house. When students complemented me on my clothes and accessories, I would go to downtown Los Angeles, and buy wholesale items to sell at my beauty school. It was totally against the school's policy to solicit, yet many of the staff bought hair accessories and jewelry from me.

I have come a long way from Santa Monica College to now, having my own hair product line and owning a beauty salon. I'm not bragging or boasting about my accomplishments. I am simply telling you this to inspire and encourage you to stay in the fight and never give up on your dreams!

<u>NOTES</u>

<u>WHERE TO START</u>

Finding the right salon that fits your style and personality can be daunting but you have to start somewhere. You may even salon hop until you come across a salon that you feel comfortable working in.

First, you must figure out what you want to get out of a salon. If you want to specialize in hair color, get with a salon that specializes in that so you can learn how to be the best. I advise to start as an assistant and be the best damn assistant there is. Make sure there is room for growth. Some bosses will keep you stagnant without any intention of moving you up. If that becomes the case, work at another salon.

I would recommend touring salons-as many as you can! Just call up and ask the owner or manager if you can get a tour, meet the staff, see the salon traffic, and ask as many questions as possible. After touring salons, you will find one that stands out to pursue working for.

First impressions are very important. When I'm considering a new employee to join our team, I pay attention to body language and how the candidate communicates orally. Here are a few tips for new employees:

- Dress sharp and clean. It shows that you take pride in the way you look.

- Be on time for interviews and for work. It shows respect for other people's time.

- Be able to take in constructive criticism

- Follow directions.

- Be friendly…no attitudes allowed.

- Have a flexible schedule. Willing to work!

The hardest thing about owning a salon, is having the right people working for you. Many people can't grasp the concept of work ethic. The grind is real!

Before I owned my salon, I worked for many hair salon owners, and what I've learned were the good ways and the bad ways to run a business. The best way to learn how to be an entrepreneur is through experience. One must obtain a certain level of experience to be an exceptional boss. You must acquire the willingness to work hard and be disciplined. You have to be a team player. Knowing how to manage your money will keep you from making desperate decisions that can damage your business. So take care of yourself and Mind Your Business.

Make a habit of absorbing the skills and knowledge you need to become a success in your business. There is only so much you can get out of a book. Obtaining real life experience is priceless….There is nothing like it!

BELIEVE IN YOURSELF

Everyone thought that boxing champ, Floyd Mayweather, was crazy for thinking that he could make $200 million in one fight. He kept putting that crazy notion into the universe by telling his team and friends. So you can imagine the victory he felt when he and others witnessed his dream become a reality when Manny Pacquiao and he fought on May 2, 2015, and he made $200 million in one night.

Before you begin any business, you have to truly believe in yourself and know that you can be successful. Determination and tenacity are key elements to being a successful business owner. Adapting a positive mental attitude is vital in every aspect of your career. It's not an easy road, but it is most rewarding when you can control your own money flow.

Stop being lazy and do the work! I can always tell the broke from the wealthy just by their conversation. A broke person complains all the time, and puts the blame on everyone for their mishaps. They are too lazy to get out of their rut so they give up. The wealthy are problem solvers. It doesn't matter whose problem it is, you better believe… it will get fixed. Instead of complaining, the wealthy will put in the necessary work to make their situation better.

Sometimes you just have to go with your gut and do what you feel. Don't worry about everyone else opinions about what you need to do. It's okay to get constructive criticism, especially if it comes from a genuine place but you have to be the one that is satisfied with your final decision.

If you don't believe in yourself, who will? There is a sense of confidence you must have in order to be successful. Believe that you can pull it off, even if people doubt you. It starts from the heart by having love and passion for your craft. The more you practice, the more you become confident.

Even if you feel that you are not where you want to be in your career, love department, or in life, still have gratitude. Be thankful for what you do have. Try not to take things for granted. As long as you keep waking up in the morning, you will always have a chance to turn your negative situation into a positive one. Where you want to go is your decision. And your decision should be made today! If you feel that you are not ready for success and the challenges that comes with it, then I suggest you stop reading this book and work on freeing yourself from fear.

EACH ONE: TEACH ONE

Find yourself a positive mentor with a teachable spirit. Lolita Goods, who I call, the "Queen of Weaves", was an exceptional mentor for me. She made a deep impact in my life by grooming me to be a better stylist but most of all she impressed me with her impeccable work ethic. I assisted Lolita at the first hair salon I worked at called, "Platinum Cuts" in Studio City, California. It was owned by rapper, Napoleon from The Outlawz and his brother Moonie. We spent days at the salon where we would start working at 6:00 a.m. and clock out by 2:00 a.m. The work was definitely tasking. There would be about 7-8 weaves a day for us to tackle, but no matter how many times I would break down crying - I never gave up.

Before attending Cosmetology school, I was a braider at Platinum Cuts. When I didn't have clients, I would assist Lolita in braiding her clients for weaves, taking down weaves, wash and blow dry. I was able to learn firsthand how to install natural-looking sew-in weaves and other tricks of the trade, that people would pay thousands of dollars to learn. Lolita wasn't stingy with sharing the knowledge. In fact, we went into business together after I graduated from the Cosmetology program in 2005. We devised a plan in my kitchen on how to execute our own hair extension workshop all around Southern California. We taught Cosmetology students and salon professionals several hair extension techniques at our hands-on-workshops.

Have you heard the axiom," fake it 'till you make it"?
Well, that's sort of how Lolita and I started Hair Escapades
Ultimate Hair Extension Workshop. We didn't read a book
or take a class on how to start it, but we had a sense of what
students would expect and want. We put ourselves in the
student's shoes. Our first workshop was truly a success and
we just got better and better with each one we held. The
moral of the story is sometimes you just have to step out on
faith and take a risk. If you don't try then, how are you
supposed to know?

DO YOUR RESEARCH

You should never invest your money in something that you know nothing about. No matter who referred you or how good it sounds coming from a fast talker. Forever and always…you still have to do your own research. Gather information from the Internet, read books and attend seminars. Maybe take a class that will help with the business you are investing in rather it be a beauty salon, beauty products or anything in the beauty business. You can possibly intern or work for a company that is in your same field so you can get the experience of how to run your own. Observe successful people and study their formula on how they became successful.

When I decided it was time to develop my own organic shampoo and conditioner…what took up most of my time was the research. I spent countless hours looking at, "how to" YouTube videos on how to make homemade beauty products. I wanted to know what ingredients moisturize the hair and what essential oils promote hair growth. Having a keen sense of smell helped with the scent of my product. I remember going to Whole Foods and testing each essential oil to see what would complement my product.

A huge part of your research should be focus or consumer groups that can test out your product. They are able to give you their honest opinions without being biased. Because I am a hairstylist, my focus group happened to be my clients. My assistants and I were able to test my product out on them while they were getting their hair washed at the salon.

We were able to test our shampoo and conditioner on them to see the results on different hair textures and the clients gave us their reviews.

When I was contemplating expanding into a bigger location, I spoke with my junior high school friend, Monique, owner of The Hair Café salon. She gave me some really great advice on what clauses I should add to my leasing agreement for my salon. (I share those tips later in the book) For example, I asked for three free months to give myself breathing room as I prepare my salon before opening. I also had a few conversations with my homeboy, Doc the Barber, who owns DK barbershop down the street from my recent location. He had his shop for over 5 years, which is why it was a great opportunity to pick his brain. The greatest advice he gave me was to start small and simple; not to over extend my finances. Get the basics to start with and do more as I make more money. He shared, "At least have it clean and ready for work".

What better way to get advice from people who have already done what you are trying to do? They can tell you what works and what doesn't. This next portion of the chapter is a worksheet. Feel free to discuss these questions with a friend, mentor or write it down in your career journal.

- Study your competition: Name three entrepreneurs in your field you admire.

- Observe successful people: Who do you personally find

successful? Is this a family member? A public figure? Best friend? What is it about this person that makes them successful?

- Know your craft: Educate yourself!

- How can I brand myself?

- What's my niche? What am I good at? What do people rave about when it comes to my work? What do you feel the most confident doing?

- What makes me different from the rest? How am I unique?

- What makes my brand unique?

- What's my target market?

- What steps do I need to fulfill my goal?

<u>NOTES</u>

BE CONSISTENT AND STAY PERSISTENT

The first time I took the State Board Cosmetology test, I failed miserably. Surprisingly, I passed the written test which was harder than Chinese arithmetic, but failed the practical. How could this happen when I studied so diligently? I even paid to take a class to prepare me for the test two times and I still failed. What had happened was, I ran out of time. Every time I forgot a step, I would run to the sink and wash my hands to give myself time to figure out the next step. As I was in the parking lot of the building, on the phone with my mom crying like a newborn baby, I thought about quitting. My mom talked me down from the ledge and told me to brush myself off and try again. After I wiped my tears away, I paid the $50.00 to retake the test once more.

A couple of months later, I went back and passed the practical test with flying colors. You would have thought I won the lotto the way I zipped up and down the hallway screaming and yelling in excitement. The moral to this story is to never give up. Be persistent at winning! Just because you failed once, twice or multiple times doesn't mean you give up. Behind every success story is failure.

While I was in Cosmetology school, I built a side business selling accessories to students, patrons and teachers at the school. I took it up a notch by starting an online boutique called, AMBERESCAPADES.COM. This was back in 2004 before online boutiques were even popular like how they are now. I sold purses, hair accessories and a few homemade t-shirts. I had it for about a year and gave up on it. Boy, I wish I would have been patient enough to develop it because I'm pretty sure it would have been a huge success. I didn't give it a chance to grow and blossom.

 Consistency and Persistence…If you have these two main ingredients in your success stew, you can never be stopped. They will all wonder why you are so successful but little do they know it is the consistency of your hard work and quality of service. Never back down from anything or anyone. You are persistent at getting things done and getting what you want accomplished.

You have to be consistent in the level of quality you give your customers. Quality is more important than quantity. And with the internet being a major marketing tool, there is no room for mistakes. One or two bad reviews online can possibly ruin your business. You will be surprised at what your customers will pay attention to without you even noticing. I have gained so many new clients because of previous hair stylists, who they had been loyal to for years but began to get lazy and stopped being consistent with the quality of work and service that was once provided.

I've witnessed some business owners spend the majority of their profit on themselves and let their business suffer. When the money starts rolling in, they become greedy and start to lack consistency in the quality of their business. They let their ego lead them to believe that clients won't leave them no matter what or how they treat them. It's sad to see these type of stylists' self-destruct. Keep your head in the game and do the right thing!

<u>NOTES</u>

SAVE YOUR MONEY TO SAVE YOUR ASS

"It doesn't matter how much money you have…you can always spend it all…"

My Jewish Black Mother

Excuses are for losers! I've heard almost every excuse of why a person does not save her/his money. It does not matter if you are working for minimum wage or earning six figures. Get into the habit of paying yourself first. Make a commitment to yourself on how much money you will be able to save weekly. You can start as low as five dollars for every client that sits in your chair and when you get comfortable enough to save more, then you add it to your account.

Initially, you may not have the discipline to save your money on your own but there is a way to pay yourself automatically. Set up an automatic payment with your bank where they can withdraw a certain amount of money from your checking and deposit into your savings… weekly or monthly. Save your money so you don't have to kiss anyone's ass. Stop being a desperate broke bitch. The one who puts up the money is the one who calls the shots. They say you should use other people's money to invest but sometimes it's better to invest your own so you will be in control. It cuts out unnecessary confusion.

Fixing your credit will save you tons of money because, the better your credit, the lower your interest rate will be when purchasing a car, a house or getting a loan for your business. There are two options: You can try fixing your credit yourself, or get legal aid from a credit consultant.

Nine times out of ten, you have to acquire a decent credit score in order for the owner to trust you renting a space for your business.

Delay Gratification: Don't be so quick to spend all of your money buying things instantly. Sometimes, you have to hold back and think things through before making that purchase. It's tempting to spend when you receive cash in hand on a daily basis. Trust and believe that the devil will sit his evil ass on your shoulder and try to convince you to spend your hard earned money on frivolous items that won't make you any money in return. There are sacrifices to make if you sincerely want to become wealthy and it may mean to hold back from getting that new expensive car or the latest designer handbag.

There are a few celebrity hairstylists who I used to aspire to be like. In my early stage of my career, I watched them drive expensive cars, own upscale hair salons in prominent areas such as Beverly Hills. They went through millions of dollars and then ended up losing everything to go right back where they started from. If I didn't learn anything, I learned to always save my money. Don't think that you can't have any fun. By all means, enjoy life but manage your money wisely in the process. Eventually, you get old and tired and the money may not come as often. So, it's better to be prepared. Make wise investments so your money works for you.

NOTES

CHALLENGE

Save at least $5.00 from each client that sits in your chair. You can always deposit more but it has to be at least $5.00. You will be surprised at how much that adds up. For each sew-in weave or big color job you do, save $10.00

If you have direct deposit, you can have your bank automatically transfer money into your savings account. If you cannot make budgeting a lifelong habit, then it will be impossible to achieve financial independence. The more money you save the more people will try to take from you.

Money hungry vultures come out of the woodworks persuading you to invest in projects or businesses that you don't have any knowledge of. Some family members and friends will nickel and dime your ass to death, especially if they know that you are exceptional at saving your money. I know that a lot of people have a hard time with being disciplined with saving their money but that is the main component to help catapult your business and keep it alive. Set yourself up in a way where if there is an emergency you have the funds to solve your problem.

Here is the game:

- Set up an emergency savings account for just your unexpected emergency expenses. For instance, if your car breaks down. If your blow dryer or flat iron goes out and you need to purchase a new one.

- Once you've saved $1,500 in your emergency account,

take $500 out and set up an Amnesia account. There should be no withdraws coming out of this account. "Just forget about it!" in my Italian accent.

- At least once a week, there should be money going towards your amnesia and emergency account.

- Purchase real estate

DOING BUSINESS BEYOND YOUR MEANS

Have you heard of the phrase, "living beyond your means"? Well, the same applies to starting a business. Don't do business beyond your means. Build as you go. I wouldn't suggest borrowing a huge sum of money from the beginning of your business ventures especially if you haven't made any money yet. It's okay to dream big but don't create debt before you start your business or it could fail before it even starts.

If you are a baker and have plans to open a bakery, sell baked goods around town; to family and friends, in stores, at farmers' markets and other events. You still have to test the market first and see what's popular and what flops before investing a huge amount of capital. Play smart!

Make the money first and get your brand out to the universe. Once you build up enough cash flow then you can possibly get a storefront, that is affordable. If you can handle it, take out a small loan to help with added expenses to get started.

Many years ago, I worked for a salon owner who took out over $120,000 on a business loan to open up her hair salon. Let's call her Alice. The majority of the loan went towards the renovation and the furniture. She had about 10 booths and only four or five of them were occupied. Alice struggled because of the overhead and emergency expenses that she didn't take into account. Not only was she in debt, but she was a horrible boss; a control freak. So, it was difficult to keep those booths occupied when hairstylists would quit because they couldn't deal with her over-bearing behavior. Eventually, she sold the salon and moved to a salon suite.

In comparison, I did the exact opposite. First, I became a manager at a salon which gave me experience at being a boss. I had double duties because I was working as a hairstylist too. Once I was able to get my clientele up, I moved to a salon suite, which was a great way for me to branch out on my own without the burden of a hefty overhead that a storefront salon would bring. At a salon suite, the water, electric and other bills are included in the rent. So, I was paying $300 a week which is about the same as paying booth rent at a salon but you are working in privacy without the hassle of the typical salon drama.

Each salon suite already has a shampoo bowl and styling chair. The suite was equipped with cabinets and shelves for retail. You have the ability to decorate it as you please. You are still a salon owner but on a smaller scale. Yes, you are still required to have licenses and permits for your suite like any other legitimate business.

Four years later, when I outgrew my salon suite, I felt it was time to make a move. My commercial agent Leslie was able to find a storefront that fit my budget. At first the search was hard because Leslie had to look for a property space that was already equipped with the plumbing and electrical outlets. My location had to have great parking to make it convenient for my clients and employees.

Finally, the search was over when she came across a nice sized salon space on Ventura that already had three shampoo bowls hooked up, plumbing, and electrical outlets connected. That ended up saving me about $10,000.00. There is also free gated parking in the back.

If you can, get into a location that used to be a salon- one that already has outlets, and plumbing established; you're winning! I set up a budget of what I was going to spend and I pretty much stuck to it. I used an app on my phone called Pinterest which gave me great decorating ideas for less. I was able to create a modern-cozy salon without going over the top. You can go on Craigslist for used salon furniture too. A lot of times there are salons going out of business that sell tools and furniture.

NOTES

CREDIT AND LOANS

Because I had decent credit, the owner approved me for my salon space in Tarzana, CA. Later, I found out from Leslie that a lot of people who wanted to rent a space from the same building I leased, got turned down because their personal credit score was too low. Notice, how I said personal credit and not business credit. I don't care what an advisor tells you about business credit. If they say that your personal credit doesn't matter, they are dead wrong.

I have a LLC Corporation and my personal credit was still checked by banks, other lending institutions and credit card companies even though the money was for my business.

To avoid spending all of my savings, I decided to take out a small business loan of $5,000 that I could afford to pay down on each month. I used it mainly for the section deposit, first and last month rent on my salon. The remaining balance, I used for the washer and dryer, salon furniture, and so on.

The bottom line is to use a loan as leverage for your business. Don't use a loan to buy the latest Gucci purse or to buy bottles at the club to try to impress strangers. Use the money to flip into producing more money. Notice with my testimony that I took baby steps and allowed myself room for growth. A lot of us have champagne taste on a beer budget. Control your spending urges before it becomes an appetite for disaster.

<u>NOTES</u>

TOO LEGIT TO QUIT

Whether you have a salon suite or a storefront, you must acquire the necessary permits and licenses to run your business legitimately:

- Cosmetology or Beautician License: No beauty salon can service customers without a licensed beautician or hairstylist present. A valid cosmetologist's license issued in the state where the salon is located must be posted in full view on the interior wall of the store during business hours or anytime a customer is present. All workers in the shop must also hold a license or be currently enrolled in an accredited program that will lead to a beautician or cosmetologist license issued by the state. Operating a salon without a license on display or allowing unlicensed workers to serve customers can result in fines and the loss of the salon owners' license.

- Business License: your salon business will require a business license issued by the secretary of state where the shop is located. The license must be renewed annually in most cases, and notification of the business creation must be announced for a period of two weeks in a local newspaper or other designated publication. Your valid business license must be posted in a visible position on an interior wall of the shop at all times.

- Tax ID: a tax ID is required by the local, county, or State government in most cases. Tax ID numbers are provided by the Department of Taxation that governs the area where the business is located. Tax ID's provide your business with the permissions required to collect and submit sales tax on every transaction made in the salons. Sales taxes are typically calculated and submitted on a quarterly basis although some states don't have them at all. If your state does, no retail or service business that deals with the public and sells product through a storefront or other retail space can operate without one.

- Business insurance: Business Insurance is essential for any salon to have in place before opening to serve the public. Business insurance protects beauty salon owners from being sued by clients for any number of liabilities including injuries that occur on the premises or loss of equipment due to theft. Business insurance is also required by many localities and state governments for certain types of businesses, especially those that involve worker-client contact, such as hair and nail salons. I would suggest adding Property Insurance, to protect any stolen or damaged items.

  - LLC: To keep your salon business finances separate from your personal liabilities, you should obtain a limited liability corporation license from the state where your salon is located. You must perform a name search to ensure that no other business has taken the name you prefer. Once completed, the LLC must be filed with the Secretary of State and a fee paid. You must create an outline of the business organization that lists the officers of the company and their roles select one partner as the contact for all legal and business paperwork and issues.

Always have a lawyer on speed dial to check any contract or paperwork. I use a pre-paid paralegal service that I pay monthly for any business dealing that requires signing any contract. I work the hell out of some hair, even performed miracles but I knew I needed to hire certain experts to implement tasks that I couldn't carry out.

After careful negotiations with my leasing agreement for my salon space, I made sure that I had a lawyer pick through the contract with a fine tooth comb. Twenty-five pages of small print can give a busy woman like myself a serious headache. By the way, when negotiating a deal, ask for whatever you want. You may not get everything you desire, but as the saying goes, 'A closed mouth don't get fed'. In my deal, I demanded that no other hair salon can lease in the building. I asked for three free months of rent so I would have some breathing room with my finances while I set up my salon. And guess what? My prayers were answered. The owner agreed to the majority of my terms.

<u>NOTES</u>

PAY THE LADY

Make it convenient and easy for your customers to hand over their money. Have more than one way of accepting payments such as PayPal, a credit card merchant service and cash, of course. Have shipping options for customers who live too far to buy products at your salon. Make it so simple for your clients to pay you that they have no excuse for not buying your products and services.

I remember years ago, working at a salon that did not accept credit card payments. I missed out on so much money and add-on services because some clients didn't have enough cash. They only had a credit card. From that experience, I vowed to always have multiple forms of payment so I would never be put in a predicament where a client could not pay. It is so simple to take forms of payment…you can swipe a credit card from your phone using SQUARE. You can check with your bank about their credit card merchant service. I recommend that you research to find out the lowest percentage rate for each credit card transaction.

You can even have an ATM machine at your salon and get paid off each transaction by charging a fee to use the ATM. There are a lot of nail shops that use one.

If you are selling hair products and tools, make sure the inventory is organized and stocked. The worst case scenario is when a customer wants to hand over money for a product and you don't have it available. You forgot to reorder! Another bummer is when your client asks for an added service but you don't have the color or relaxer in stock. Money lost. Have a systemized way of keeping your stock organized.

If you have an online boutique, please ship products to customers in a timely fashion.

IF YOUR BUSINESS IS NOT ONLINE…GO KILL YOURSELF

I cannot begin to tell you how important it is for you to promote your business on social media and other promotional platforms. Remember back in the day, when the tell-a-friend referral was popular? Now, the majority of customers Google from their phone the nearest and best beauty salons in their area. Yes, we live in a technology age where consumers are getting referrals from off the internet. With just one click of a button, you can find a great business or a horrible business online. Even the Yellow Pages are online.

There are websites such as Google and Yelp.com that gives ratings and reviews of businesses. New and old clients should be informed by a staff member that if they enjoyed their services at your salon, write a positive review. Five star reviews benefit your business immensely. It ensures potential clients that they will get quality service. Hair Escapades has gained so many new clients from Yelp.

Potential clients have gravitated to our Five Star reviews and positive comments. http://www.yelp.com/biz/hair-escapades-los-angeles

If you haven't already, invest in a website so that potential consumers can learn more about your beauty business and if you sell products, they can purchase from your website as well. www.hairescapades.com

With sites like wix.com, they make it so consumer friendly that your child can build a website. What's really cool is, if you need some guidance, you can call Wix technical support and they will help guide you through the editing process. Because the majority of consumers are more on their phone than their computer, you have to make your website mobile friendly. To get more information on customizing your website for all mobile devices…Google it!

For those of you who aren't computer savvy, hire someone to build and run your website. If you are on a strict budget, you can always do an internship with a college student who needs credits for their class.

Use social media like Facebook, Instagram, YouTube, Snapchat, Periscope, and others to promote your business. Stay consistent in posting material that relates to your business. Please don't make the mistake of posting a bunch of non-relevant bull crap because it confuses your audiences. I've seen some hairstylists post nothing but fighting videos and other folk's wise quotes but don't have one picture of what they do for a living. None of their work is being displayed but they complain about not having enough clients. For the sake of your business, post your work!

In 2008, I created my YouTube channel: Hair Escapades. www.youtube.com/hairescapades At first, I used to post videos of me free styling to instrumental rap beats. Then, I switched my focus to hosting videos of me transforming clients from drab to fab. Not only was I documenting my journey as a hairstylist but I was inspiring other stylists. It was and is still a great way to promote my business. I've had clients travel from all over the world to get their hair done by me. To show you how impactful YouTube is, I once got a call from a young lady that lived in Tokyo. She saw my YouTube videos and decided to book an appointment for a sew-in weave! She came from the airport straight to the salon with her luggage. Of course, I made a video and it's called: from Japan to Los Angeles to get her Weave Done. Now I have over two million viewers.

NOTES

LEAVE YOUR MARK

Do not solely depend on the internet to promote your business. Possessing professional business cards is still a plus when marketing your business. Wherever I go, I am always passing out my business cards or leaving them at other businesses to promote my brand. For all of my business owners; don't ever be too prideful to promote your own business. If you don't do it, who will? The best clients to grab are the ones that work behind the counter at retail stores and restaurants. They become your best advertisement. The next time you go to your favorite place to eat, leave some business cards on the table and at the front counter.

Challenge yourself on how many business cards you can give out in one week and let's see what the end result will be. It's a number game. The more cards you give out, the greater the chance you have in gaining more clients.

Before your client leaves out of the salon, give them business cards and motivate them to pass out your cards by offering them a discount when their referral gets serviced. They will greatly appreciate the kind gesture. It makes a strong lasting impression when you pass out a professional business card. Here are a few tips for designing effective business cards.

- Keeping it simple is important. Don't make your cards

gaudy with an overload of information. Simple and cleaner is the way to go.

- Make sure that your fonts are clear and easy to understand. Don't make the mistake of having the type too uncomfortably small to read.

- Include your social media, website and contact information.

- Please proofread the information on the card before it goes to print. You don't want to end up with the address or phone number wrong.

- Always have business cards with you at all times. Keep some in every purse. Reorder in a timely fashion so you don't run out.

WHAT TO DO ON SLOW DAYS

You're not going to always have busy days or a busy week and waiting for the phone to ring is not the answer to filling up your schedule. Complaining about your week definitely will not help you. Keep in mind to always be a problem solver. Here are a few tips that I use when there are slow days.

- Pass out business cards, flyers or any marketing material around the neighborhood: shopping malls, grocery stores, coffee houses, colleges and so on. Before approaching a potential client, have a script prepared that is short, sweet and to the point. What I do to catch their attention is offer a discount if they schedule an appointment.

- Text or email clients who have not booked in a while. Offer them a discount if they book on your slow day. There is salon software like SalonIris that can send out your promotional campaigns to your clients in the database all at once.

- Post on all of your social media informing clients that they will receive a discount if they schedule an appointment that day.

- If you have a lot of foot traffic outside of your salon, stand in front and meet clients by greeting them with a smile and a business card. Invite them inside of the salon for a tour and offer them a drink or a snack.

Implementing these great ideas will surely keep you busy to the point where you don't have to worry about another slow day. Like anything worth having, you must put in the work!

CUSTOMER SERVICE

Treat your clients the way you want to be treated. It's an easy concept but so many stylists don't want to apply this in their salon. As soon as a client walks through our doors, they are greeted with a smile- "Welcome to Hair Escapades…" One of my lovely assistants then offers them a beverage or snack that we keep in stock. It's the simple things that count. We carry the latest fashion and hair magazines for our clients to thumb through while getting serviced.

It's a great idea to have a client book where you store all of their pertinent information including birthdays, hair color formulas and I like to customize their favorite things. For example, I have a client that loves pink Starburst candy. I have my assistants pick through the Starbursts to gather a few of them for her appointment.

Listen to your client's needs and wants. If a client expresses to you that they want only a trim, please don't go Edward Scissorhands crazy by giving them the big chop. Even if your client needs more of her split ends cut, explain the benefits and get approval from her/him first before cutting more. They will gladly appreciate it.

Don't ever develop an attitude where you feel like it's a privilege to sit in your chair. Check your ego at the door. The moment you think that you can treat a client any old kind of way is the moment you lose them. Stay humble! Keep a clean station and salon. "Cleanliness is next to

Godliness", as it says in the Bible.

RESPECT TIME AND IT WILL RESPECT YOU

Respect other people's time. One main reason why I've been successful with keeping clients is because I am punctual for appointments. When I know that I may be running late, I'm courteous enough to tell my clients that I'm running behind or I will have my receptionist/assistant contact them. If I schedule clients back to back, I have my assistants to help with my work flow so my clients will not have to wait no longer than fifteen minutes to get serviced. At Hair Escapades, we schedule clients depending on what they are getting done.

I've gained so many new clients because their previous hairstylists didn't respect their time. Stylists would double or triple-book having their clients waiting all day, just for a service that takes only an hour to do. No one has time for that nonsense, especially in this impatient computer day and age. It's truly a blessing to be customarily booked but you have to know when to bring in an assistant to aid with the load. I never could understand how some busy stylists choose to work without an assistant; coveting all the money, not wanting to share. Little do they know, not only is their business suffering from trying to do all the work, but it's hard on the body and soul. Do the opposite of what losers do. Be on time!

Here are a few helpful tips for being punctual:

- Set your watch, clock, and time on your phone 10 minutes ahead.

- Prepare the night before. Pick out your clothes and have them already ironed. Prepare your lunch.

- Set an alarm for when you have to wake up in the morning and for when to leave the house.

- Track how long tasks take so you have a general idea of its timing.

- Use your online calendar

ANSWER YO DAMN PHONE

After you've set up shop and have your doors open for business, you must answer your phone. If you're unavailable, hire a receptionist, an assistant or a virtual assistant. If you happen to miss a potential client's call, please return their call within 15 minutes to avoid losing them to another stylist. Take into account that you must train whoever answers your phone to speak in a professional manner. You've implemented marketing and promotions in your business so when they call, you must answer. Here are some important tips when answering the phone.

- Smile, so when you are speaking it sounds pleasant. Sound excited and happy to help your potential customer.

- Find out how the customer found out about your business so you can keep track of which marketing platform is working. If they were referred from another client, give the referred a discount on their next service to show your appreciation.

- Patiently, answer any and all questions. If you need to place them on hold, ask them first. When you get back on the phone, thank them for holding.

- When you schedule their appointment, ask them to spell their name so it is correct when you add them in the scheduling system. Get their primary telephone number and email address.

- Once, you get the client's name, use it at least three times during the phone conversation. Whenever they call you again, use their name. It's a considerate gesture. It makes them feel important.

- Make sure you take the call in a quiet place so the client can hear what you are saying clearer and vice versa.

- Don't talk fast or sound like you are rushing because you can make the client feel like you don't have time for them. Be clear and precise so they can understand everything you are saying.

At our salon, we get a lot of compliments from new clients about how nice we are over the phone. When you are pleasant over the phone, it reassures the client that you can be trusted and it makes them feel at ease. A lot of times, they've called several salons before you and they get some really rude receptionists so you must set yourself apart by doing the complete opposite; be nice.

BAD ASSOCIATIONS SPOIL USEFUL HABITS

1 Cor. 15:33

"They hate you not because you are better than them but because you try harder than they do. You work harder than they do and you care more than they do. -Katt Williams

Don't let toxic relationships and negative people distract you from accomplishing your goals. People can plant negative seeds in your head to make you doubt yourself, only if you let them. I deliberately ignore phone calls from certain negative people because I know that they have a sob story to tell. They are always negative and negativity brings about illness, depression and insomnia; just to name a few. Misery loves company and I refuse to be a guest at a miserable person's pity party.

There is nothing wrong with trying to support people but once you realize that you are wasting your time with those who are not ready to help themselves then, it's time to walk away.

THEY ARE JEALOUS OF YOU BECAUSE YOU'VE EXCEEDED THEIR EXPECTATIONS OF YOU.

As you began this journey toward financial freedom, remember that everyone may not share your happiness. It's lonely at the top. You begin to feel a disconnection between some of your friends because you don't hang out like you used to. While your friends are at the club, you are at home in front of your computer building your brand.

When everyone is sleep, you are awake, thinking on how to take your business to the next level.

You find it difficult to relate to people who don't save their money and who don't want to learn how to. They burden you with their mishaps. Listening to their complaints, wears on your spirit. You start to develop a no-tolerance-for-bullshit policy.

Surround yourself with self-motivators, movers and shakers. It's stimulating to the soul to have conversations with winners as oppose to gossiping all day about frivolous things. Have a mentor: one that is understanding and patient, knowledgeable and experienced, who isn't selfish with sharing.

"It's not that you've changed. It's the people around you start to change and act funny towards you." -Jay Z

Stay rich in spirit and love what you do. Everything else will fall into place. Being happy starts within. Personally, I have to be in the right state of mind to be able to generate the kind of money I need to sustain my family's lifestyle. I don't have the time or energy for negative drama. I would rather be by myself than to be surround myself with negative-miserable people. Even though my job requires catering to my clients; I understand that I have to also cater to myself and make sure that I'm happy. If you are truly passionate about what you do, don't worry…the money will come. See you at the top!

THE END...

FOR NOW...

www.ingramcontent.com/pod-product-compliance
Lightning Source LLC
Chambersburg PA
CBHW070359190526
45169CB00003B/1044